Windows on the Maghrib...

TRIBAL AND URBAN WEAVINGS OF MOROCCO

Editors:

JEFFERSON S. HYDE   JANICE HARMER
MIRIAM LORIMER   W. RUSSELL PICKERING

This catalog is published in conjunction with the exhibition
"Windows on the Maghrib...Tribal and Urban
Weavings of Morocco"

The Frank H. McClung Museum
The University of Tennessee, Knoxville, Tennessee
February 29-April 5, 1992

Guest Curator — Jefferson S. Hyde

Co-Published by

THE FRANK H. McCLUNG MUSEUM, The University of
Tennessee, 1327 Circle Park Drive, Knoxville, TN 37996
and
THE NEAR EASTERN ART RESEARCH CENTER, 4200
Cathedral Ave., N.W. (Suite 1112), Washington, D.C. 20016

Printed by Keith Press, Knoxville, Tennessee

Typesetting and graphics by Hart Graphics,
Knoxville, Tennessee.

Textile color photography by Bernhard Schopper,
Alexandria, Virginia

© 1991 by The Frank H. McClung Museum, The University of
Tennessee, Knoxville, TN and The Near Eastern Art Research
Center, Washington D.C. All rights reserved.
No part of this publication may be reprinted without permission in
writing from the publishers.

Excerpt from In Morocco, copyright © 1971
by Faith Mellon Willcox, reprinted by permission of
Harcourt Brace Jovanovich, Inc.

ISBN 1-880174-02-2

Frank H. McClung Occasional Paper No. 11

Contents

DIRECTOR'S NOTES   2
Jefferson Chapman, Ph.D.

ACKNOWLEDGEMENTS   3
Janice Harmer and Miriam Lorimer

INTRODUCTION   4
Alex Haley

PROLOGUE   5
Ambassador Mohamed Belkhayat
Embassy of the Kingdom of Morocco to the United States
and
Ambassador Michael Ussery
Embassy of the United States to Morocco

WEAVING MAP OF MOROCCO   6
William Fontanez

"WINDOWS ON THE MAGHRIB…
TRIBAL AND URBAN
WEAVINGS OF MOROCCO"   7–9
Jefferson S. Hyde
and
W. Russell Pickering

"THE THREADED NEEDLE"   10
P. Lynn Denton

COLOR PLATE COMMENTARY
W. Russell Pickering
and
Jefferson S. Hyde
STRUCTURAL ANALYSES   11–42
P. Lynn Denton

WEAVINGS AND
LENDERS TO THE EXHIBITION   43–44
Jefferson S. Hyde

BIBLIOGRAPHY   45–46
James R. Jereb, Ph.D.

Director's Notes

Jefferson Chapman, Ph.D.

THE UNIVERSITY OF TENNESSEE and the Frank H. McClung Museum are honored to host Windows on the Maghrib: Tribal and Urban Weavings of Morocco and to co-publish this catalog. Like the proverbial acorn from which mighty oaks grow, the exhibition evolved from a small display to an internationally significant event. For this, I must thank the editors of this catalog. I have worked closely with Jan Harmer and Mim Lorimer and they are to be commended for their vision, drive, and hard work. Combined with the talent and expertise of Jefferson Hyde and Russ Pickering, the project came to fruition. My thanks also go to those donors and lenders mentioned elsewhere whose generosity and interest made it all possible.

Principal among the elements of a museum's mission is education. Morocco and its arts and culture are little known or appreciated by the vast majority of the citizens of this country. In bringing together these splendid examples of weaver's art, we facilitate understanding and a better appreciation of this rich North African culture. It is hoped that the exhibition and catalog will stimulate interest and continued scholarly research in the fiber arts of Al Maghrib Al Aqsa.

Jefferson Chapman, Director
The Frank H. McClung Museum

Acknowledgements

Janice Harmer and Miriam Lorimer

IN A PROJECT of this scope, many people have contributed knowledge, time and enthusiasm. Their expertise and effort have put this catalog in your hands.

We are very grateful to Harold and James Keshishian who were instrumental in providing a receiving area for photography of the rugs, storage, and space for structural analysis.

Special thanks to Lynn Denton who spent countless donated hours analyzing the physical structure of the rugs and textiles. Dr. James Jereb, through his extensive knowledge of Moroccan textiles, supplied a most complete bibliography. William Fontenez of the University of Tennessee's Geography Department created a unique weaving map of Morocco.

We are very grateful to Alf Taylor who provided many "Treasures of Morocco" (visual artifacts) for the catalog and exhibition. These added dimension and depth to a view of Moroccan life.

This catalog could have not been possible without financial support of several organizations and a number of individuals. The Near Eastern Art Research Center was instrumental in providing support and the Moroccan Rug and Textile Society also gave generously towards this fund. Royal Air Maroc contributed for the catalog cover. Individuals who contributed were: Mrs. Myrna Bloom, Mr. Peter Davies, Mr. Dennis R. Dodds, Dr. Charles S. Grippi, Ms. Hilary Harts, Mr. and Mrs. Harold M. Keshishian, Mr. and Mrs. T.R. Lawrence, Ms. Brooke Pickering, Mr. W. Russell Pickering, Dr. and Mrs. William T. Price, Dr. Paul F. Ryan, Mr. and Mrs. Alf Taylor, Mr. and Mrs. Raoul Tschebull.

Dr. and Mrs. Joseph Harb and Mr. and Mrs. Sam Jubran of Knoxville, TN provided invaluable local support of the exhibition.

Finally, we extend out deep appreciation to Dr. Jefferson Chapman and the staff of Frank H. McClung Museum for their sincere interest and enthusiasm shown in every stage of development of the exhibition and catalog.

Janice Harmer and Miriam Lorimer, fine arts consultants, originated the concept for this Moroccan exhibition, and served as organizers, coordinators, and co-editors of the catalog.

Introduction

Alex Haley

MY INVITATION from the office of King Hassan II to visit his kingdom of Morocco certainly met with no delay on my part. Both before and during the long flight to Casablanca, I read all the books and pamphlets I could about the country whose name alone had always conveyed to me an image of exotica. I was aware of the old saying that most things are more exciting in anticipation than in fact. But this was an exception, for nothing I'd read had managed to convey what my next two weeks presented in visual, and cultural and spiritual impacts of Morocco.

Now, five years and four Moroccan visits later, I could share much about the Moroccan food, especially my favorite *tagine* dishes which are baked within the native earthenware pots. I could exude about Morocco's marvelous hotels, my pick as the most unforgettable among them being the Mamounia in the wondrous city of Marrakech. (The famed small North African country's cosmopolitan Marrakech somewhat compares to our San Francisco, as their political Rabat is like our Washington, D.C., and their commercial Casablanca is something similar to our Chicago; we have no equivalent of Morocco's religious city of Fes.) It's no wonder why the Mamounia Hotel was where Winston Churchill loved to visit and paint his canvases.

Oh, I could go on and on about the *souk* marketplaces where probably whatever you might want is sold, and the more rigorously you learn to bargain, the more you will win respect. I could rhapsodize about the religious temples which are busy with the worshipping of the faithful, from the first streaks of dawn when the day's first prayers are cried out in the haunting tones of the *muezzin*.

As you can likely gather, I could go on and on. But for this special event, I must tell you that what captivated me above all, what developed my bargaining skills to their highest degree, was the Moroccan artistry in weaving.

I visited, first, the government schools where apprentices were being trained who clearly felt nothing less than a reverence for their looms. Later on, I was was taken to the private homes of some among Morocco's most acclaimed master weavers, whose carpets and textiles adorned the museums and the palaces. And I must tell you now that I know of no better way for you to appreciate Moroccan weaving than if you will visit the major exhibition of textiles at the Frank H. McClung Museum at the University of Tennessee in Knoxville. The materials on display have been drawn from a broad range of private and museum collections of the finest of examples from every major weaving area within Morocco.

Alex Haley

Alex Haley

Alex Haley is an author/lecturer and Pulitzer Prize winner for the book Roots.

Prologue

Embassy of the
Kingdom of Morocco
Washington, D.C.

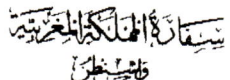

Mohamed Belkhayat, Moroccan Ambassador to the United States

I AM DELIGHTED as Ambassador of the Kingdom of Morocco to the U.S.A. to introduce the American public to "Windows on the Maghrib, Tribal and Urban Weavings of Morocco".

This book gives a right assessment of the great artistic beauty and cultural diversity which Morocco enjoys through its various kinds of weavings. It will certainly contribute to a better understanding in America of my country and its people who are characterized by noble, ancient and colorful traditions, warm hospitality and openness to other cultures. This is due in particular to its location in the crossroads of Europe and Africa, the Atlantic Ocean and the Mediterranean Sea. As a cultural melting pot, Morocco has so much to offer for both students of art and civilization, and for welcome visitors. May this achievement help to increase the cultural exchange between the U.S.A. and Morocco.

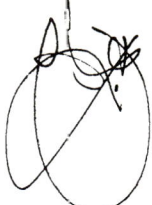

Mohamed Belkhayat
Ambassador

Michael Ussery, U.S. Ambassador to Morocco

EMBASSY OF THE UNITED STATES OF AMERICA
RABAT, MOROCCO

DURING MY THREE YEARS as Ambassador to Morocco, I have been continually fascinated and repeatedly surprised by the beauty of Moroccan textiles. Morocco has a unique and clearly identifiable artistic tradition dating back to the days of the Moorish empires. This vision finds its greatest expression in the decorative arts, where Morocco has nurtured a tradition of craftsmanship and continues to produce works of extraordinary beauty. Moroccan artisans have produced superior ceramics, woodwork, brass, textiles and carpets that are well known and respected throughout the Moslem world and Europe.

All Moroccan crafts have ancient origins, but carpet weaving is probably the oldest. The rural carpets reflect the landscapes of the regions where they are made. Some imitate the brilliant colors of Morocco's flowers, some display the beige and tan tones of the desert, while others capture the snow white and jet black of the mountains. Urban carpets, particularly from Rabat and its sister city, Salé, were introduced into Morocco more recently — in the 18th century. These carpets combine a harmony of colors with a multitude of designs, some of which are said to be magical, and bring to mind garden paths around a central pool. I hope that exhibits like this one, by exposing people to some of Morocco's cultural riches, will help introduce more Americans to Morocco.

Michael Ussery
U.S. Ambassador to Morocco

Weaving Map of Morocco

Windows on the Maghrib...

TRIBAL AND URBAN WEAVINGS OF MOROCCO

Jefferson S. Hyde and *W. Russell Pickering*

As it descends to the horizon, the Moroccan sky does not gently mute its color as our skies do; the blazing blue of the zenith continues down to the clear sharp line where sky meets earth. Its intensity heightens the color of everything seen against it—white parapets, a tawny boulder in silhouette, a black cypress throwing a long ellipse of shadow. No wonder North Africa has driven painters mad with desire to capture it on canvas. From Reubens to Delacroix, Matisse, Klee, they have tried to convey that unbelievable brilliance—the lacquer crispness of the magentas, oranges, pinks, scarlets... the spear of a century plant stabbing the sky, its low, sharp leaves curling back to earth... a turquoise jay flashing on tan wings. All colors are sharp-edged, unambiguous, in air which seems to have been polished to a sheen. Only the shadows are subtle—in them lurks every tone the eye can register.[1]

MOROCCO POSSESSES great geographic, cultural, and artistic beauty superimposed upon a long and colorful heritage. This heritage began with the ancient Berber tribes. It broadened at the end of the seventh century as the conquering Arab armies swept across North Africa past the Straits of Gibraltar to the Atlantic coastline. This conquest would mark the western limits of the Moslem world for a thousand years, and Morocco would be known as Al Maghrib Al Aqsa, The Far West.

Because the invaders focused their attention on the riches of Spain and southern France, a hundred years passed before a nation began to take form with the arrival in northern Morocco of Moulay Idriss, a fugitive descendant of the Prophet Mohammed. Idriss encouraged the conversion of the Berber tribes to the Moslem faith, but it was left to his son, Idriss II, to lay the foundations of Fes as an "imperial city" and to establish The Idrissis as the first of six major dynasties which have ruled Morocco to the present day.

The great artistic beauty and diversity which Morocco enjoys is nowhere more apparent than in the refined art form displayed by the weavings produced throughout the country. There are four main weaving groups in Morocco: the commercial looms of the cities, the rural Arab tribes in the central region known as the Plains of Marrakech, the Berber tribes of the High Atlas Mountains in the south, and the Berbers of the Middle Atlas to the north and west. (Map pg. 6) Each group employs overall pattern concepts, designs, color tones and weaving techniques which dramatically distinguish one from the other. In addition, Morocco possesses a proud tradition of embroidery which is produced primarily in the larger cities of the north and is based on design elements

---

[1] Faith Mellen Willcox, IN MOROCCO, Pg. 46, Harcourt, Brace, Jovanovich. 1971

drawn from Andalusia and the Middle East.

The primary weaving techniques include the Senneh, Gordes, and Berber knots (the latter used exclusively by Middle Atlas

Figure A
(From left to right)
Senneh, Gördes and Berber knots

tribes) for carpets, and for the knotted pile areas which decorate the flatweaves (Figure A). The plain weave and split tapestry tech-

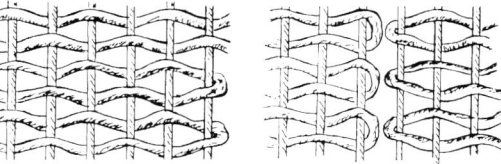

Figure B
(From left to right)
The Plain Weave and Split Tapestry Techniques

niques (Figure B), and skip plain weave (Figure C) are employed in the non-pile, or flatwoven, examples produced for everyday

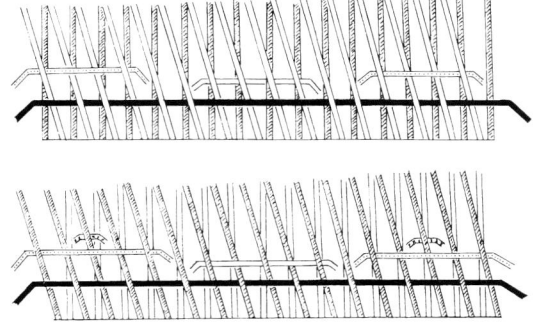

Figure C
Weaving sequence of skip plain weave

use and ceremonial occasions. These include floor coverings, beds, blankets, capes and shawls, animal trappings, tent dividers, tent bands and straps, bags and pillows.

It is the women who execute the woven art form and it is, in part, through this medium that they can express their talents and creativity. There is a great interest in, and some controversy about, the symbolism employed by the Berbers in their weavings. Tribal weavers often use terms such as saw, female snake, bone of a snake, tongue of a female snake, leaf of bamboo and others in referring to their geometric renditions. Anthropologists and historians may legitimately debate the origin of these symbols, but many of the weavers do believe in their own interpretations of the meaning of the designs they use.

Within the tribes it is apparent that there is a certain vying among the weavers. In fact, the weaving talents of a young girl always have been a very considerable factor in her desirability as a bride. This friendly competition brings a significant contribution to home and family as an expression of pride and joy of creation. Many of the weavings, particularly saddle covers, belts and bags are displayed in public to reflect the status of the family.

Best known among the urban carpets are the Rabats, traditionally produced on commercial looms in the modern national capital, Rabat. These weavings using the Gordes knot have a thick pile and are patterned after Turkish rugs (Plate 1). Another traditional urban carpet was made in the small town of Mediouna, twelve miles east of Casablanca where both Turkish and Persian designs were used (Plate 2). Today, factories and cooperatives produce the "modern" Rabats, rugs with Mediouna motifs, white carpets with heavy pile known in the trade as "Berbers", and flatweaves from the towns of Oued-Zem and Tiflet.

The area between Casablanca and Marrakech, known as the Plains of Marrakech or The Haouz, encompasses the textiles from the three major Arab weaving tribes: The Oulad Bou Sbaa, Chiadma and Rehamna (Plates 3-5) and from the area around the town of Boujad (front cover). The knotted pile carpets are distinguished by their red fields, multicolored aprons, black weft-elongated triangles along the sides, and in the case of the Oulad Bou Sbaas (Plate 3), the use of a symmetrical design and motifs taken from the Rabat carpets. Others present free and random patterns (Plate 5). The flatweaves employ designs and techniques also found in Algeria and Tunisia. The Plains of Marrakech is the only region in Morocco where the slit tapestry technique is used (Plate 3 and front cover). During the French Protectorate (1912-1956), a commercial group of carpets developed in and around the town of Chichaoua which resembles the Bou Sbaas in color but tend to be more loosely woven with fewer field designs that often contain representational figures.

Beyond Marrakech, among the peaks of the High Atlas and the semi-desert areas beyond, the tribal confederations produce weavings which are as distinctive each from the other as they are from the rest of Moroccan pieces. The pile rugs of the Ouaouzguite Confederation are made throughout the area with the major activity now centered around the market town of Tazenakht (Plate 6). These rugs contain bright colors with geometric central medallions and many Rabat border elements. Particularly interesting features are the multi-colored weft panels found on the back of many of the pieces.

AN ATTRACTIVE and popular sub-group of flatweaves, and also flatweaves with a knotted pile are known as "Glaouas" after the tribe which controlled the region until Independence in 1956 (Plate 7). To the south the tribes in the area of Mt. Siroua produce finely woven capes, bags and belts (Plates 8-9). To the north Ait Haddidou and related sub-tribes weave some of the most dramatic and attractive women's shawls made in Morocco (Plate 10).

The many tribes of the Middle Atlas produce a wide variety of weavings that are justifiably famous for their originality of patterns and excellence of execution. One of the reasons is the use of the skip plain weave which produces intricate patterns unique to the Berbers in this region. Design elements rely heavily upon diamonds, half-diamond motifs and other geometrical designs employed in a series of horizontal panels. A particularly interesting feature, also unique, is the use of a "reverse pile" whereby the weaver regards the side with knotted pile as the back of the piece.

The best known examples include those produced by the Zaer, Zaiane, Beni M'Guild, Beni M'Tir, Ait Youssi, Marmoucha, Beni Ouarain and Beni Saddene Confederations and tribes (Plates 11-19). In recent years an important new group of weavings has developed named for the market town of Azrou, sixty miles south of Fes. These pieces combine traditional design elements and colors of the surrounding tribes into a sort of collage of Middle Atlas weavings (Plate 20).

The Zemmour Confederation inhabits a long plateau that stretches from Meknes west to Rabat. Their weavings (Plates 21-29 and back cover) are distinguished by a variety of bright colors, strong red fields, widespread use of a symmetrical design concept, and vertical columns with designs created by small multicolored diamonds. In addition, the saddle covers, saddle bags, ceremonial blankets and pillows are generally regarded to be some of the finest weavings in Morocco.

In 1787 Sultan Mohammed III and President George Washington signed what has become the longest unbroken Treaty of Friendship in American history. Despite this friendship and the remarkable variety of the material, Morocco and its art, ceramics and weavings are still relatively unknown in this country. A goal of this catalog, and the exhibition on which it is based, is to develop a better understanding of the arts of Morocco and to introduce the viewer to a rare opportunity that exists for those who love learning and beauty.

Jefferson S. Hyde, Santa Fe, N.M. has studied extensively the weavings and cultures of Morocco

W. Russell Pickering, Washington, D.C., Co-editor of FROM THE FAR WEST: RUGS AND TEXTILES OF MOROCCO, and Chairman of the Near Eastern Art Research Center.

The Threaded Needle:

HISTORIC MOROCCAN EMBROIDERY

P. Lynn Denton

THE HERITAGE OF embroidery in Morocco reflects the complex movement of Islamic and non-Islamic peoples across North Africa, Spain, and throughout the Mediterranean basin. Motifs, design organization, and stitch techniques reflect this interaction although the specific processes of interaction and exchange are not known. Refugees from the Christian "reconquista" of Spain, Portuguese occupation of portions of the coastline, expansion pressures from the Turkish empire, and French colonial administration singly and collectively influenced the character and practice of embroidery in Morocco during the last four to five centuries. Representative examples survive only from the 18th-20th centuries, however (See Plates 30-32).

Cities were the most prolific centers for producing embroidery, although women's embroidered headcoverings and garments from rural regions were illustrated by Besancenot (1942) and are documented in museum collections. Women of both Arab and Jewish communities embellished household textiles and apparel with silk and metallic thread. Articles embroidered for either private use or public distribution included soft furnishings such as cushion and mattress covers, curtains, wall and door hangings, shawls, head scarves, bath veils, tray covers and handkerchiefs. A variety of stitches including satin, buttonhole, stem, star, long armed cross, brick, plait, and double sided triangular Turkish stitch were used to create free form designs or to execute counted patterns on linen or cotton ground fabric. Distinctive color choice, design composition, and stitch selection characterizes the work from each city.

Moroccan embroidery must be viewed within a framework of trans-Mediterranean historical relationships. An exploration of the complex internal and external cultural processes which have shaped the practice of embroidery in the Maghrib may reveal important influences and connections. Particularly striking similarities can be noted with Greek Island embroideries and some Balkan examples (Trilling, 1983; Johnstone, 1972; Benaki Museum, 1980; Roberson, 1986). Irrespective of their role within the past or the present, these exquisite works created by individual hands are an expressive reminder of the personal, human scale of history.

Benaki Museum
    1980 <u>Greek Embroideries</u>. Athens: The Banaki Museum.

Besancenot, Jean
    1942 <u>Types et costumes du Maroc</u>. Paris: Horizones de France.

Johnstone, Pauline
    1972 <u>A Guide to Greek Island Embroidery</u>. London: Victoria & Albert Museum

Roberson Center for the Arts & Sciences
    1986 <u>Goddesses and Their Offspring: 19th and 20th Century Eastern European Embroideries</u>. Binghamton: Roberson Center for the Arts & Sciences

Trilling, James
    1983 <u>Aegean Crossroads Greek Island Embroideries in the Textile Museum</u>. Washington, D.C.: The Textile Museum

P. Lynn Denton, Assistant Director of the Texas Memorial Museum, The University of Texas at Austin. Mrs. Denton is currently working on her Ph.D. on weavings on Morocco.

Structural Analysis:
RABAT CARPET

warp:	cotton, 4-ply commercial (4 Z yarns S plied)
weft:	cotton, 4-ply commercial, 2 shots
pile:	wool, single S yarn, Gordes (symmetrical) knot, 7 horiz. x 7 vert. per inch (49 per sq. in)
selvedges:	plain weave over 3 warps
finish:	wool fringe, overhand knotting of 4 strands of supplementary 4 Z yarns S plied spaced by single row twined wool

Plate 1

RABAT CARPET
20th Century — 6'10" x 7'3"
American Museum of Moroccan Art Collection

This Rabat contains many of the traditional elements borrowed from Turkish carpets. There is the symmetrical pattern with floral medallion and pendants surrounded by a variety of stylized floral designs. The five borders also have motifs drawn mainly from Anatolia. Representational figures in the form of teapots have been introduced. The square size indicates the piece was woven for a modern house rather than the traditional Moroccan dwelling with rooms of oblong dimensions.

Structural Analysis:
MEDIOUNA CARPET

warp:	wool or goat hair, ivory, 4 5-yarns Z-plied
weft:	wool, magenta, single Z-and 2 S-yarns Z-plied, 5 shots
pile:	wool or goat hair, 3 or 4 S-yarns, Senneh (asymmetrical) knot open on left, 7.5 horiz. x 4 vert. per in. (30 per sq. in)

Plate 2

MEDIOUNA CARPET
20th Century — 4'11" x 7'9"
Harold and Melissa Keshishian Collection

Although they present a format of central medallions on fields limited by several borders similar to the Rabats, carpets from Medoiuna employ distinctive field designs and color combinations. Here, a central white medallion and two green and red octagonal medallions with lateral pendants are flanked by stepped triangular motifs. These elements are probably inspired by carpets from northwest Persia. The endless design concept in the field is contained by four major and minor borders with stylized flowers drawn from Turkish carpets.

Plate 3

OULAD BOU SBAA CARPET
20th Century — 4'11" x 15'10"
W. Russell Pickering Collection

Structural Analysis:
OULAD BOU SBAA CARPET

warp:	goat hair, tightly spun single Z yarns
weft:	wool, single Z yarns
technique:	mixed-weft face plain weave with split tapestry bans, wedge weave bands, and knotted pile
pile:	wool, 2 Z yarns S plied, Gordes (symmetrical) knots, 8 horiz. x 6 vert. per inch (48 per sq. in.)
selvedges:	goat hair, single Z yarn weft reinforcement over 3 sets of 3 Z warp yarns S plied
finish:	twisted warp loops held by twined goat hair separating cord at cloth beam end; cut warps grouped in variable numbers, plaited, and knotted at warp beam end

This "Bou Sbaa" combines elements from several adjacent areas to and within The Plains of Marrakech. The symmetrical pattern as well as the designs in the knotted pile areas are derived from Rabat. The motifs and split tapestry technique employed in the flatwoven panels are found in Algerian and Tunisian textiles and reflect the Arab heritage of the tribes which inhabit the plains.

Structural Analysis:
CHIADMA CARPET

warp:	wool, single Z yarns
weft:	wool, single Z yarns, 1-2 shots; 3-5 shots between design breaks
pile:	wool, loosely spun single S yarns, Berber knot, 3 horiz. x 3 vert. per inch (9 per sq. in); variable pile height according to pattern area
selvedges:	supplementary band of wool single Z yarns in plain weave over 3 groups of paired commercial cotton yarns; attached by overcast stitch with wool single Z yarns and 2 Z yarns S plied
finish:	wool, single Z yarns; 2 strand twining at cloth beam end; 2 rows uncountered twining at warp beam end; supplementary fringe of 2 Z yarns S plied, paired and knotted

Plate 4

CHIADMA CARPET
20th Century — 6'4" x 11'8"
Mohamed El Maarouf Collection

Chiadma weavings are distinguished by their bright and varied colors and "freedom of design." These characteristics are emphasized in this example by three levels of pile: the closely cropped black, the medium length greens and yellows, and the longer burgundy areas. Another interesting feature is the use of two symmetrical patterns: the two opposing horizontal panels at either end each containing a large diamond surrounded by multicolored triangles, and the center vertical panel flanked by two opposing vertical panels with similar patterns.

Structural Analysis:
REHAMNA CARPET

warp:	wool, natural gray, 2 Z-yarns S-plied
weft:	wool, orange and purple, 2 Z-yarns S-plied, multiplied wefted (up to 15 shots)
pile:	wool, 2 Z-yarns, Gordes (symmetrical) knot (double row; above: knotted over 4 warps, progressively overlapping 2 warps; below: knotted over 2 warps no wefting between these two rows). 5 horiz., pile bands are more than 1 in. apart
color:	(7) orange-red, purple, orange, black, white, pink, gray
finish:	bands of weft-faced plain weave both ends, fringe of braided warps upper end
selvedge:	brown wool or goat hair, 4 cords of 2 warps attached by selvedge wrapping extending 4 in. into body of rug at 4 in. intervals

Plate 5

REHAMNA CARPET
20th Century — 6' x 8'2"
Ralph S. Yohe Collection

Unlike rugs from neighboring areas to the east and south, Rehamnas employ abstract designs and asymmetrical patterns. This example uses a technique composed of multiple rows of knots placed between several rows of wefts. Oblong blocks and lines of colors are created which produce a wild, almost overwhelming abstraction, a sort of "Paul Klee of Moroccan carpets". The piece narrows sharply as it ascends due to the inability of the weaver to secure the sides during the weaving process.

Structural Analysis:
OUAOUZGUITE (TAZENAKHT) CARPET

warp:	wool, 2 Z yarns, S plied
weft:	wool, single Z yarns, 8 shots
technique:	weft face plain weave with knotted pile
pile:	wool, single Z yarns, Gordes (symmetrical) knots, 6 horiz. x 4 vert. per inch (24 per sq. in.)
selvedges:	supplementary 4 warp group attached to 4 warp selvedge group by Oriental stitch join
finish:	cut warps at both cloth and warp beam ends

Plate 6

OUAOUZGUITE (TAZENAKHT) CARPET
19th/20th Century — 4'6" x 11'7"
Alf and Judi Taylor Collection

Carpets from this region generally employ a geometric medallion superimposed upon a bright orange/yellow or blue field with patterns of endless designs limited by one or more borders. This example has a medallion with a diamond motif upon a field containing a variety of geometric elements. Several borders surround the field, the inner border displaying a series of colorful camels. Other animals and teapots appear at either end of the field. This symmetrical format with medallion and confining borders reflects influence from Rabat and the Middle East. The foundation wefts were dyed in several shades to produce multicolored horizontal panels on the back of the piece.

Structural Analysis:
OUAOUZGUITE (GLAOUA) CARPET

warp:	goat hair, single S yarns
weft:	wool, single Z yarns; 2 Z yarns S plied for twining
technique:	mixed-weft face plain weave with knotted pile, 2 strand twining
pile:	wool, 2 Z yarns S plied, Gordes (symmetrical) knots, 5 horiz. x 3 vert. per inch (15 per sq. in.)
selvedges:	plain weave over 2 groups of 4 warps
finish:	twined separating cord at cloth beam end; braided fringes each within 3 groups of 4-5 warp ends at warp beam end

Plate 7

OUAOUZGUITE (GLAOUA) CARPET
20th Century — 4'8" x 12'6"
T.R. and Linda Lawrence Collection

"Glaouas" are some of the most colorful and versatile weavings in Morocco. In this example, a knotted pile border surrounds a symmetrical field containing knotted pile bands which flank areas with geometric patterns. These alternate with black and white flatwoven panels the latter displaying triangle elements executed in knotted pile.

OUAOUZGUITE MAN'S CAPE

Not available for structural analysis.

Plate 8

OUAOUZGUITE MAN'S CAPE
20th Century — 9' x 4'6"
James F. Jereb Collection

These rare pieces are among the most spectacular weaving in Morocco. A black plainwoven field surrounds a long oval red space containing embroidered designs believed to represent sun and lizard symbols. The geometric elements along the edges are also found on the walls of Berber structures in the area.

Structural Analysis:
OUAOUZGUITE (SIROUA) WOMAN'S SHAWL

warp:	wool, tightly spun single Z yarns
weft:	wool, single Z yarns, patterning in 2 Z yarns S plied; cotton, single Z yarns, patterning in 3 Z yarns S plied
technique:	mixed-weft face plain weave with supplementary weft float patterning, discontinuous weft brocading, countered 2 strand twining
selvedges:	plain weave over 2 groups of 4 warps
finish:	4 cut warps grouped and tightly wrapped with single wool Z yarn from base to tip at both cloth beam and warp beam ends; supplementary warp fringe incorporated in wrapping

Plate 9

OUAOUZGUITE (SIROUA) WOMAN'S SHAWL

20th Century — 2'11" x 7'4"
Lamdaghri Med Ben Cherif Collection

A finely woven, cream-colored base decorated with bands of white cotton and embroidered designs are characteristic of weavings from the Siroua region in the High Atlas. Delicately twirled, multicolored fringes at either end complete these pieces.

Structural Analysis:
AIT HADDIDOU WOMAN'S SHAWL

warp:	wool, single Z yarns
weft:	wool, single Z yarns, some paired
technique:	weft face plain weave, discontinuous weft brocading at selvedges
selvedges:	plain weave over 2 groups of 4 warps
finish:	4 warp ends grouped and tightly wrapped from base to tip by single wool Z yarn at both cloth beam and warp beam ends

Plate 10a

AIT HADDIDOU WOMAN'S SHAWL
20th Century   —   3'10" x 5'6"
Peter and Laurie Lese Collection

Structural Analysis:
AIT HADDIDOU WOMAN'S SHAWL

warp:	wool, tightly spun single Z yarns
weft:	wool, single Z yarns; cotton, 2 Z yarns S plied
technique:	weft face plain weave with countered 2 strand twining
selvedges:	plain weave over 2 groups of 4 warps
finish:	2 groups warp ends each of 4 Z yarns S plied are replied Z and knotted at cloth beam end; 2 groups warp ends each of 4 or 6 Z yarns S plied are re-plied Z and knotted at warp beam end
embellishment:	supplementary plaited wool fringes knotted through selvedges; 2 wool ties braided of 3 Z yarns S plied

Plate 10b

AIT HADDIDOU WOMAN'S SHAWL
20th Century   —   4' x 5'4"
W. Russell Pickering Collection

The Ait Haddidou tribes inhabit the area where the High and Middle Atlas Mountains come together on a desolate plain 8,200 to 9,800 feet above sea level half way between Marrakech and Fes. The shawls employ bands of repeating colors and shades enlivened by narrow colored strips of countered twining. White areas separate the colored panels and the selvedges are decorated with small patches of color.

Structural Analysis:
ZAER SADDLE COVER

warp:	wool, single Z yarns
weft:	wool, single Z yarns; cotton, paired 3 ply commercial; silk, paired 2 S yarns Z plied
technique:	weft face plain weave with weft substitution
selvedges:	plain weave over 1 group of warps
finish:	cut and uncut warp loops at cloth beam end; 2 Z warp ends S plied are knotted together and 3 of these groups are re-plied Z
embellishment:	widely spaced horizontal and vertical rows of single silk Gordes (symmetrical) knots; sequins

Plate 11

ZAER SADDLE COVER
20th Century — 3' x 5'
Ralph S. Yohe Collection

This example, like other weavings of the Zaer Tribe, resembles those of the Zaiane Confederation to the east. The field is composed of a series of horizontal panels with diamond and half-diamond motifs drawn in rust, reds and purples. However, the use of the bluish-green throughout the piece distinguishes it from the neighboring tribes. Double rows of multicolored triangles form the outer borders and silk tassels with sequins decorate the face.

ZAIANE CARPET
Not available for structural analysis.

Plate 12

ZAIANE CARPET
20th Century — 5'10" x 9'4"
Ralph S. Yohe Collection

This carpet is representative of knotted pile rugs from the Zaiane Confederation with an overall format of large diamonds dominating a reddish-orange field surrounded by multiple borders containing additional diamonds and half diamond motifs. These pieces are intended for use as bedding as well as floor covering, hence the long thick pile which in many examples completely obscures the design patterns. They are unique in that the weavers regard the non-pile side to be the front of the carpet.

Structural Analysis:
ZAIANE TENT DIVIDER

warp:	wool, loosely spun single Z yarns
weft:	wool, single Z yarns; cotton, tripled 3 ply commercial
technique:	weft face plain weave with weft substitution
selvedges:	plain weave over 1 group of 6 warps
finish:	separating cord of twined 3 Z yarns S plied at cloth beam end; groups of 4-5 warp ends in overhand knot with adjacent group, ends to back, at warp beam end
embellishment:	knotted pile tufts, 8 cotton yarns and paired wool yarns in Gordes (symmetrical) knots around 4 warps, alternately paired

Plate 13

ZAIANE TENT DIVIDER
20th Century — 3'10" x 10'11" (Section)
Hafidi Mohamed Collection

Tent dividers decorate the inside wall of the tent and also separate the interior into separate living spaces. The complete piece measures 22'1". It contains 8 panels with variations of the diamond and triangle motifs separated by rows of multicolored wool and white knotted pile cotton tufts. Narrow skeleton-like patterns form the borders on either side.

Structural Analysis:
BENI M'GUILD/BENI M'TIR FLATWOVEN RUG

warp:	wool, single Z yarns and sections of 2 Z yarns S plied
weft:	wool, single Z yarns; cotton, tripled 3 ply commercial
technique:	weft face plain weave with weft substitution
selvedges:	plain weave over 4 groups of 2 warps
finish:	wool, 2 Z yarns S plied, twined as separating cord with 3 spacing rows of 2 Z yarns S plied at cloth beam end; groups of 6-8 cut warp ends knotted to form fringe at warp beam end

Plate 14

BENI M'GUILD/ BENI M'TIR FLATWOVEN RUG
20th Century — 5'3" x 12'7"
William Alfred Pickering Collection

To the north of the Zaiane, the Beni M'Guild and Beni M'Tir Tribes inhabit adjacent areas on either side of Azrou, an important market town located 60 miles south of Fes. Their flatwoven pieces are sufficiently similar to make exact provenance problematic. The purple/brown panels with diamond and half-diamond motifs are associated with what are usually regarded as Zaiane and Beni M'Guild. The brighter, multicolored areas that contain skip plainweave squares with transparent designs are thought to be woven by the Beni M'Tir.

Structural Analysis:
**BENI M'GUILD/
BENI M'TIR FLATWOVEN RUG**

warp:	wool, tightly spun single Z yarns
weft:	wool, single Z yarns; cotton, paired 3 ply commercial
technique:	weft face plain weave with weft substitution
selvedges:	plain weave over group of 4 warps
finish:	wool, 3 Z yarns S plied, twined as separating cord with single 4 Z yarn S plied spacing cord at cloth beam end; fringe created by 2 groups of adjacent warp ends 4 Z plied S, re-plied Z and knotted at warp beam end

Plate 15

BENI M'GUILD/ BENI M'TIR FLATWOVEN RUG
20th Century — 5'1" x 9'2"
Peter Davies Collection

Wide panels containing unusual six pointed star — like devices are superimposed in a "transparent" fashion upon alternating plainwoven red and blue areas. Bands with geometric designs separate these wider panels and help create the symmetric pattern. The transparency feature with red and blue colors showing through the white designs, as well as the similarity in technical analysis, place this piece among the Beni M'Guild/Beni M'Tir Tribes.

Structural Analysis:
AIT YOUSSI COVER

warp:	wool, single Z yarns
weft:	wool, single Z yarns; cotton, single Z yarns and tripled 3 ply commercial; silk, 3 Z S plied
technique:	weft face plain weave with weft substitution
selvedges:	plain weave over 4 sets of 4 Z yarns S plied
finish:	single S yarn twined separating chord at cloth beam end; groups of approximately 24 warp ends braided and knotted at warp beam end
embellishment:	widely spaced horizontal and vertical rows of single Gordes (symmetrical) knots of 4 Z silk S plied; 3 Z rayon S plied; 2 Z yarns S plied commercial cotton, individually or paired; and 4 strands of 3 ply commercial cotton; sequins

Plate 16

AIT YOUSSI COVER
20th Century — 4'11" x 9'10"
Haj Mohamed Lalou Collection

Examples of Ait Youssi weavings from the Eastern Middle Atlas are rare and are known for the use of lively colors. In this piece multicolored strips of plainweave separate the bands with intricate geometric designs. Narrow vertical columns of white supplementary wefts and multicolored tufts enliven the field. Overall balance is achieved through a central panel which is flanked by six panels, the outer two at either end containing similar designs.

Plate 17

MARMOUCHA CARPET
20th Century — 5'4" x 7'2"
Brooke Pickering Collection

Structural Analysis:
MARMOUCHA CARPET

warp:	wool, loosely spun single Z yarns
weft:	wool, loosely spun single Z yarns, single shot
pile:	wool, Berber knots, single Z yarns, 3 horiz. x 4 vert. per inch (12 per sq. in.)
selvedges:	plain weave over 2 groups of 3 warps
finish:	uncut warp loops self plied S at cloth beam end; 6 warp ends knotted and groups of 3 braided at warp beam end

The Marmoucha Tribe inhabited some of the highest areas of the eastern Middle Atlas which may account for the heavy pile employed in the few known knotted pile examples. This piece is particularly interesting in that the design and color format present two carpets. The top half contains three panels with diamond devices of varied shapes and sizes and borders with "zig zag" design. Colors are vivid and the green areas are clipped short to provide relief in the pattern. In contract, the two panels in the bottom half display large similar diamond motifs. There is a very narrow black border and the colors are subdued.

Structural Analysis:
BENI OUARAIN CAPE

warp:	wool, single S yarns
weft:	wool, single S yarns; cotton, 3 ply commercial
technique:	mixed-weft face plain weave with countered 2 strand twining and discontinuous weft brocading
selvedges:	plain weave over reinforcing 4 S warp yarns Z plied
finish:	no original ends (contemporary hemming of raw edges)

Plate 18a

BENI OUARAIN CAPE
20th Century — 3'2" x 6'8"
Peter Davies Collection

Structural Analysis:
BEN OUARAIN CAPE

warp:	wool, single Z yarns
weft:	wool, tightly spun single Z yarns; cotton, 3 ply commercial
technique:	weft face plain weave with weft substitution
selvedges:	plain weave over 4 warps of 3 Z spun yarns S plied
finish:	cut warps at both cloth and warp beam ends

Plate 18b

BENI OUARAIN CAPE
20th Century — 2'10" x 7'6"
Jefferson S. Hyde Collection

The two examples displayed in Plates 18a & b are among the finest weavings of the Middle Atlas. In 18a, panels with complex geometric designs alternate with bands executed in white wool and cotton. Long ends of ivory wool weft cover the back. 18b also contains bands of geometric designs, but these alternate with plainwoven black, blue and maroon strips. Both pieces enjoy overall balance which results from the symmetrical patterns used.

Structural Analysis:
BENI SADDENE CARPET

warp:	wool, single Z yarns
weft:	wool, single Z yarns, 4 shots
pile:	wool, 2 Z yarns S plied, Gordes (symmetrical) knots, 5 horiz. x 5 vert. per inch (25 per sq. in.)
selvedges:	plain weave over 2 warps of 4 Z yarns S plied
finish:	at cloth beam end - twined separating cord of 5 Z yarns S plied and countered 2 strand twining of 2 Z yarns S plied; at warp beam end - 2 Z warp ends are S plied, tied in groups of 3 and re-plied Z; countered 2 strand twining of 2 Z yarns S plied

Plate 19

BENI SADDENE CARPET
20th Century — 5'9" x 11'4"
Alf and Judi Taylor Collection

This example is representative of the carpets of the Beni Saddene Tribe from the mountains east of Fes. Sizes are relatively large and the pile is relatively short. Purple, brown and yellow/orange are the dominant colors. Format is asymmetrical with multiple horizontal panels which contain diamond and half-diamond designs interspersed with crosses, animals and human figures.

Structural Analysis:
AZROU FLATWOVEN RUG

warp:	wool, single Z yarns
weft:	wool, single Z yarns; cotton, paired 3 play commercial
technique:	weft face plain weave with weft substitution
selvedges:	plain weave over 2 groups of 4 warps
finish:	at cloth and warp beam ends: 16-18 warps braided with 6 supplementary commercial 3 Z yarns S plied, self and supplementary tassels
embellishment:	cotton and silk Gordes (symmetrical) knotted tufts; sequins on each strand of 3 Z silk S plied attached to surface in modified (wrapped twice) Spanish knot (?)

Plate 20

AZROU FLATWOVEN RUG
20th Century — 4'10" x 11'2"
W. Russell Pickering Collection

The symmetrical pattern contains five panels with the diamond motifs which are characteristically employed by the Middle Atlas Tribes. These in turn are separated by narrow panels of oblong sections with diamond designs flanked by tufted rows of cotton and silk. The side borders are composed of columns of joined diamonds set upon a white lattice-like design. Sequins and colorfully braided tassels, respectively, decorate the field and either end.

Plate 21

ZEMMOUR CARPET
20th Century — 5'9" x 10'11"
Alf and Judi Taylor Collection

Structural Analysis:
ZEMMOUR CARPET

warp:	wool, single Z yarns
weft:	wool, single Z yarns, 2 shots
technique:	mixed - knotted pile, weft face plain weave apron with weft substitution
pile:	wool, single S yarns, Gordes (symmetrical) knot, 5 horiz. x 7 vert. per inch (35 per sq. in.)
selvedges:	supplementary selvedges of plain weave over 3 groups of 3 Z wool yarns S plied attached by Oriental stitch join
finish:	twined separating cord and spacer of 4 Z yarns S plied at cloth beam end; individual strand of commercial wool braid attached at warp beam end

Zemmour carpets traditionally have a symmetrical pattern containing a series of horizontal panels with geometric designs set upon a deep red field. Borders are generally lacking in many of the older pieces. The use of bright yellow, blue and green colors in this piece is a characteristic of knotted pile carpets.

Structural Analysis:
ZEMMOUR FLATWOVEN RUG

warp:	wool, tightly spun single Z yarns
weft:	wool, single Z yarns; cotton, paired 3 ply commercial
technique:	weft face plain weave with weft substitution
selvedges:	plain weave over single group of 6 warps
finish:	supplementary 2 Z wool yarns S plied added to warp loops and re-plied Z to form fringe at cloth beam end; 2 Z warp ends S plied, knotted in groups of threes and re-plied Z to form fringe at warp beam end
embellishment:	sequins attached by loops of 2 S silk Z plied

Plate 22

ZEMMOUR FLATWOVEN RUG
20th Century — 5'6" x 11'6"
Abdelmajid Rais El Fenni Collection

The field is composed of narrow horizontal bands with geometric designs separated by red plainwoven areas. Symmetry is achieved through three sets of staggered vertical columns which dominate each half of the piece and flank a central panel with columns containing white and dark red joined triangles. The designs in all of the vertical columns are achieved through a sort of "mosaic" technique consisting of multi-colored triangles, a process unique to Zemmour weavings.

Structural Analysis:
ZEMMOUR FLATWOVEN RUG

warp:	cotton, 3 ply commercial
weft:	wool, single Z yarns; cotton, paired 3 ply commercial; rayon, 3 Z yarns S plied and paired single S yarns
technique:	weft face plain weave with weft substitution, plain weave aprons
selvedges:	plain weave over 2 groups of paired warps
finish:	cotton twined separating cord at cloth beam end; warp fringe at warp beam end

Plate 23

ZEMMOUR FLATWOVEN RUG
Recent — 5'1" x 8'10"
Hajjam Hassan Collection

During the past decade, this type of flatweave has developed in and around Tiflet, traditionally one of the main market towns of the Zemmour Confederation located between Meknes and Rabat. Designs are executed in rayon upon a wool base and many patterns are drawn from older pieces (note the multicolored triangles in the borders). In addition, representational figures have been added including animals, human figures and, in this case, mosques.

Structural Analysis:
ZEMMOUR MAN'S BLANKET/COVER

warp:	wool, single Z yarns
weft:	wool, single Z yarns; cotton, paired 3 ply commercial; silk, 2 S yarns Z plied
technique:	weft face plain weave with weft substitution
selvedges:	plain weave over single group of 6 warps
finish:	twined separating cord of 4 Z wool yarns S plied at cloth beam end; 2 single Z warp ends S plied, groups of 3 re-plied Z to form fringe at warp beam end
embellishment:	alternately paired Gordes (symmetrical) knots in single Z wool yarns, 2 Z wool yarns S plied, 4 ply commercial wool yarns, and 2 S silk yarns Z plied; tasseled 2 S cords plied

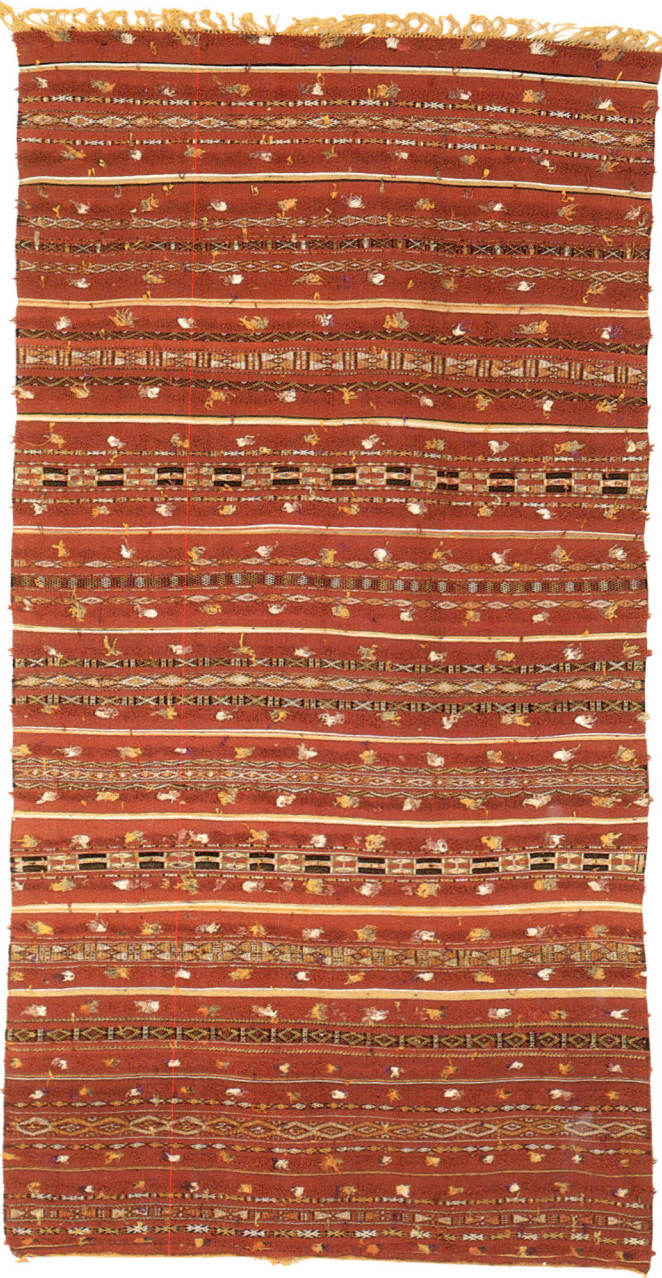

Plate 24

ZEMMOUR MAN'S BLANKET/COVER
20th Century — 5' x 9'11"
Jefferson S. Hyde Collection

These large blankets or covers are used to decorate the home during weddings, anniversaries and other ceremonial occasions. This example displays horizontal panels containing rows of geometric designs each flanked by two narrow bands with similar elements. Knotted tufts and plainwoven silk strips add vitality to the overall pattern.

Structural Analysis:
ZEMMOUR WOMAN'S BLANKET/COVER

warp:	cotton, 3 Z yarns S plied
weft:	wool, single Z yarns; cotton, single Z yarns and 3 Z yarns S plied, untwisted silk
technique:	mixed-weft face plain weave with weft substitution, countered 2 strand twining, embroidery
selvedges:	one selvedge of plain weave over single group of 3 warps; other selvedge of plain weave over 3 groups of 3 warps with 2 of the groups ending approximately 3 3/4 inches from finished edge
finish:	4 warps re-plied Z to form fringe at both cloth and warp beam ends

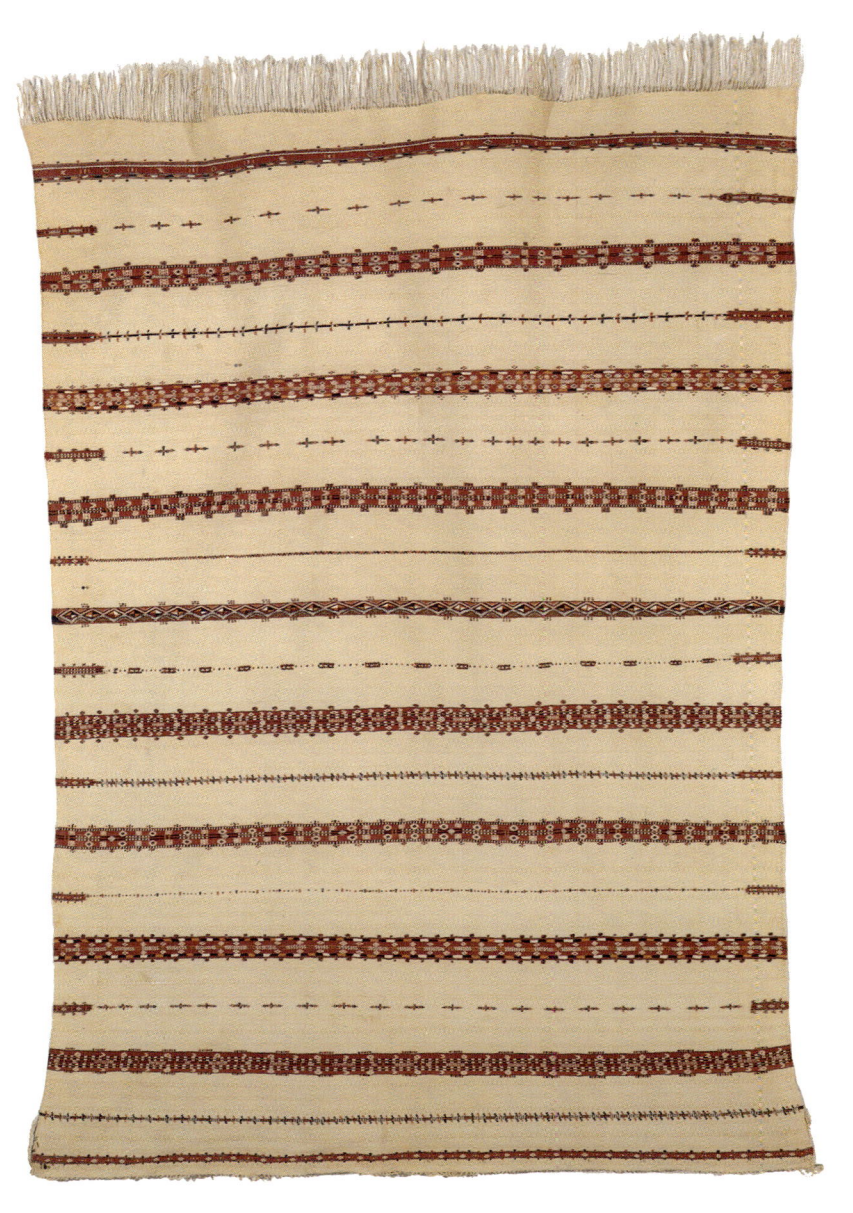

Plate 25

ZEMMOUR WOMAN'S BLANKET/COVER
20th Century   —   4'6" x 6'9"
Hilary Harts Collection

This finely woven woman's blanket or shawl was made for use as a bed cover, shawl or seat cover for special events. The panels contain varied geometric designs which cover the field. Strips of narrow elements and "shoots" of cotton enliven the cream-colored bands.

Structural Analysis:
ZEMMOUR SADDLE COVER

warp:	wool, single Z yarns
weft:	wool, single Z yarns; cotton, paired 3 ply commercial; silk, mixed - single Z strands, 2 Z strands S plied, and 2 strands Z plied
technique:	weft face plain weave with weft substitution
selvedges:	plain weave over 3 groups of 2-3 warps
finish:	at both cloth and warp beam ends hemmed by overcast stitch which attaches silk flat braid edging, supplementary braided silk fringes
embellishments:	supplementary braided silk fringes attached at selvedges; sequins on each strand of 3 S silk Z plied attached to surface with modified (wrapped twice) Spanish knot (?)

Plate 26

ZEMMOUR SADDLE COVER
20th Century — 3'3" x 5'8"
T.R. and Linda Lawrence Collection

Saddle covers of this quality were made for special occasions. The rider would dismount at his destination and spread the cover over the saddle. Upon departure it was folded and placed in a pouch for the ride home. In this example, multicolored silk bands separate panels with intricate designs. A grid work of sequins attached to silk tassels decorate the field and emphasize the decorative function of these pieces. The multicolored triangles produce a zig zag pattern in the borders.

Structural Analysis:
ZEMMOUR SADDLE COVER

warp:	wool, tightly spun single Z yarns
weft:	wool, single Z yarns; cotton, paired 3 ply commercial; silk, single S strands
technique:	weft face plain weave with weft substitution
selvedges:	plain weave over single group of 6 warps
finish:	warp loops with supplementary fringe of 2 Z yarns S plied, re-plied Z at cloth beam end; groups of 3 individual warp Z yarns S plied and re-plied Z with adjacent group to from fringe

Plate 27

ZEMMOUR SADDLE COVER
20th Century — 2'10" x 4'7"
Alf and Judi Taylor Collection

Four vertical columns are composed of small multicolored triangles which produce a joined diamond pattern. Blocks containing vertical geometric designs alternate with oblong red and yellow panels.

ZEMMOUR GRAIN BAG

Not available for structural analysis.

Plate 28

ZEMMOUR GRAIN BAG
20th Century — 4'6" x 8'6"
William Alfred Pickering Collection

Grain bags are woven and used extensively by the nomadic and agricultural tribes throughout Morocco. Because of the fine weave and attention to design and detail, this piece was probably intended to decorate the animal at ceremonial occasions. As with saddle bags and pillows, grain bags are made in one long piece with the half intended as the face executed in intricate designs and the backs in plain woven panels.

Plate 29a

ZEMMOUR SADDLE BAG
20th Century — 1' x 3'4"
Jefferson S. Hyde Collection

Structural Analysis:
ZEMMOUR SADDLE BAG

warp:	wool, single Z yarns
weft:	wool, single Z yarns; cotton, 3 ply commercial; silk, 2 S strands Z plied
technique:	weft face plain weave with weft substitution; each bag woven as single piece, joined at selvedges by over cast stitch attaching silk flat braid to cover the seam; bag openings hemmed in overcast stitch attaching silk flat braid on face; separate straps attached with running stitch
selvedges:	obscured by braid on bag; plain weave over 2 groups of 2 warps on straps
embellishments:	silk, supplementary 2 tiered plaited fringe tassels knotted to inside bag at bottom fold; evidence of surface silk tufts/tassels or sequin attachments remain on bag interior

Plate 29b

ZEMMOUR PILLOW
20th Century — 1'4" x 3'5"
Lisa Petrov Collection

Structural Analysis:
ZEMMOUR PILLOW

warp:	wool, single Z yarns
weft:	wool, single Z yarns; cotton, paired 3 ply commercial; silk, mixed - 2 S strands Z plied and 2 Z strands S plied
technique:	weft face plain weave with weft substitution; woven in one piece, joined at selvedges and warp ends
selvedges:	joined by overcast stitch attaching supplementary flat wool braid to cover seam
finish:	obscured by overcast stitch attachment of supplementary flat wool braid to cover seam
embellishment:	2 S strands Z plied tasseled silk fringe; silk and wool modified Spanish knot tufts with sequins (?)

Like saddle covers, double bags are used for special public events. They can be hung on the saddle as well as worn by the owner in the market. Generally woven in one long piece, the faces are executed with intricate designs while the backs employ simpler plainwoven panels. Pillows are made throughout the Middle Atlas for local use in houses and tents. As with the saddle bags, the faces contain carefully woven designs, often with sequins and silk or wool tassels, and the backs are executed in bands of plainweave.

Structural Analysis:
FES EMBROIDERY

ground fabric:	cotton, single Z warp and weft yarns in 38 count even weave
selvedges:	none
embellishment:	single ply silk embroidery; Algerian eye (star) stitch, buttonhole stitch, double running stitch, and triangular 2-sided Turkish filling stitch

Plate 30

FES EMBROIDERY
19th Century — 2'8" x 2'10"
Gordon and Eleanor Browne Collection

The rarest of Moroccan textiles include the blue Fes embroideries produced in the homes and local workshops in the tradition of the first Imperial Capital. They are still made in limited quantities for women's garments and to embellish the household. The cartoon in this example is reminiscent of a by-product of the Ottoman/Greek Island influence. There are four quadrants with stylized trees which emanate from a central axis. Intricately drawn triangles are wedded to the traditional Fes borders.

Structural Analysis:
TETOUAN EMBROIDERY

ground fabric:	pieced linen in 4 panels, each 34-36 count even weave
selvedges:	none
embellishment:	single ply silk embroidery; cross stitch, plaited Algerian stitch

Plate 31

TETOUAN EMBROIDERY
18th/19th Century   —   3'3" x 6'7"
Paul F. Ryan Collection

Tetouan is located 150 miles north of Fes and for centuries has been a refuge for the Moslem and Jewish populations driven from Spain after the Reconquista in 1492. This intensely colorful embroidery reflects the Andalusian heritage through the stylized flowers in each outer panel as well as the crab-like motifs in the main field. A lattice device dominates the central portion of an overall symmetrical format.

WOMAN'S DRESS

Not available for structural analysis.

Plate 32

WOMAN'S DRESS
20th Century — 4'3" x 4'
Alf and Judi Taylor Collection

This silk brocade caftan is an example of historic urban clothing. Skilled weavers in Morocco produced such fine textiles, although it is not known if this fabric was loomed locally or imported from Europe. Ornate additions of silver and silk braid trim edge the sleeves and hem. The neckline and center front opening are embellished with an applique of commercially produced silver tape surrounded by couched silver cord over stiffened fabric. The shoulder and arm seems are also ornamented with silver tape applique. A fine cotton lines the garment.

Weavings and Lenders to the Exhibition

Exhibition Number	Description	Lender	Size	Circa
	Embroideries			
1	Tetouan Woman's Belt	W. Russell Pickering	7" x 7'10"	20th Century
2°	Tetouan Embroidery	Paul F. Ryan	3'3" x 6'7"	18th/19th Century
3°	Fes Embroidery	Gordon & Eleanor Browne	2'8" x 2'10"	19th Century
4°	Woman's Dress	Alf & Judi Taylor	4'3" x 4'	20th Century
5	Woman's Dress	A.M.M.A.[1]	5' x 5'	19th Century
	Urban Weavings			
6	Oued Zem Flatwoven Rug	A.M.M.A.[1]	5' x 9'	Recent
7°	Tiflet Flatwoven Rug	Hajjam Hassan	5'1" x 8'10"	Recent
8°	Rabat Carpet	A.M.M.A.[1]	6'10" x 7'3"	20th Century
9°	Mediouna Carpet	Harold & Melissa Keshishian	4'11" x 7'9"	20th Century
	The Plains of Marrakech			
10	Boujad Carpet	T.R. & Linda Lawrence	2'5" x 6'10"	20th Century
11°	Boujad Blanket	Brooke Pickering	4'11" x 10'5"	20th Century
12°	Chiadma Carpet	Maarouf El Mohamed	6'4" x 11'8"	20th Century
13°	Oulad Bou Sbaa Carpet	W. Russell Pickering	4' x 10'7"	20th Century
14°	Rehamna Carpet	Ralph S. Yohe	6' x 8'2"	20th Century
	The High Atlas			
15	Siroua Man's Belt	Private Collection	7" x 10'1"	20th Century
16°	Ouaouzguite Man's Cape	James F. Jereb	9' x 4'6"	20th Century
17	Ouaouzguite (Taz.[3]) Gun Cover	I.M.A[2]	10" x 6'3"	20th Century
18	Ait Haddidou Woman's Shawl	Ralph S. Yohe	3'9" x 5'6"	20th Century
19	Ait Haddidou Woman's Shawl	Brooke Pickering	4'1" x 5'6"	20th Century
20°	Ait Haddidou Woman's Shawl	W. Russell Pickering	4' x 5'4"	20th Century
21°	Ait Haddidou Woman's Shawl	Peter & Laurie Lese	3'10" x 5'6"	20th Century
22	Ait Haddidou Woman's Shawl	James F. Jereb	3'5" x 5'10"	20th Century
23	Ouaouzguite (Taz.[3]) Carpet	Joseph Verner Reed	4'2" x 12'	20th Century
24°	Ouaouzguite (Taz.[3]) Carpet	Alf & Judi Taylor	4'6" x 11'7"	19th/20th Century
25	Ouaouzguite (Glaoua) Grain Bag	Private Collection	4'7" x 10'6"	20th Century
26	Ouaouzguite (Glaoua) Carpet	David & Janice Harmer	5' x 9'4"	20th Century
27°	Ouaouzguite (Glaoua) Carpet	T.R. & Linda Lawrence	4'6" x 12'6"	20th Century
28	Ouaouzguite (Taz.[3]) Carpet	Joseph Verner Reed	4'2" x 7'9"	20th Century
29	Ouaouzguite (Taz.[3]) Carpet	Dean & Joy Stockwell	4'7" x 7'	20th Century
30*	Siroua Woman's Shawl	Lamdaghri Med Ben Cherif	2'11" x 7'4"	20th Century

continued on the next page

Exhibition Number	Description	Lender	Size	Circa
\multicolumn{5}{c}{*The Zemmour Confederation*}			

Exhibition Number	Description	Lender	Size	Circa
31°	Zemmour Carpet	Alf & Judi Taylor	5'9" x 10'11"	20th Century
32°	Zemmour Grain Bag	William Alfred Pickering	4'6" x 8'6"	20th Century
33	Zemmour Flatwoven Rug	Alf & Judi Taylor	5'1" x 10'7"	20th Century
34°	Zemmour Flatwoven Rug	Abdelmajid Rais El Fenni	5'6" x 11'6"	20th Century
35°	Zemmour Flatwoven Rug	Jerry & Twila Griffith	5'7" x 10'3"	20th Century
36	Zemmour Woman's Blanket	Jefferson S. Hyde	5'2" x 9'	19th Century
37°	Zemmour Woman's Blanket	Hilary Harts	4'6" x 6'9"	20th Century
38°	Zemmour Man's Blanket	Jefferson S. Hyde	5' x 9'11"	20th Century
39	Zemmour Woman's Blanket	Bernard & Miriam Lorimer	4'8" x 8'10"	20th Century
40	Zemmour Saddle Cover	Lee R. Lyon	3'6" x 5'8"	20th Century
41°	Zemmour Saddle Cover	Alf & Judi Taylor	2'10" x 4'7"	20th Century
42°	Zemmour Saddle Cover	T.R. & Linda Lawrence	3'3" x 5'8"	20th Century
43	Zemmour Saddle Cover	Gordon & Evan Hyde	3'6" x 5'9"	Recent
44	Zemmour Woman's Shawl	Glee J. Stanley	3'6" x 6'4"	20th Century
45°	Zemmour Saddle Bags	Jefferson S. Hyde	1' x 3'4"	20th Century
46°	Zemmour Pillow	Lisa Petrov	1'4" x 3'5"	20th Century

Middle Atlas

Exhibition Number	Description	Lender	Size	Circa
47°	Zaiane Carpet	Ralph S. Yohe	5'10" x 9'4"	20th Century
48°	Zaiane Tent Divider	Hafidi Mohamed	3'10" x 22'1"	20th Century
49	Zaiane Ten Band	Ralph S. Yohe	1'3" x 45'	20th Century
50	Zaiane Woman's Shawl	Private Collection	4' x 8'8"	Recent
51	Zaiane Woman's Shawl	Hilary Harts	3'10" x 6'2"	Recent
52	Beni M'Guild/Beni M'tir Shawl	I.M.A.[2]	3'8" x 6'8"	20th Century
53°	Beni M'Guild/Beni M'tir Cover	Peter Davies	5'1" x 9'2"	20th Century
54°	Beni M'Guild/Beni M'tir Flatwoven Rug	William Alfred Pickering	5'3" x 12'7"	20th Century
55°	Azrou Flatwoven Rug	W. Russell Pickering	4'10" x 11'2"	20th Century
56°	Bani Saddene Carpet	Alf & Judi Taylor	5'9" x 11'4"	20th Century
57°	Ait Youssi Cover	Haj Mohamed Lalou	4'11" x 9'10"	20th Century
58	Ait Yacoub	Brooke Pickering	6'6" x 7'7"	20th Century
59°	Zaer Saddle Cover	Ralph S. Yohe	3' x 5'	20th Century
60°	Marmoucha Carpet	Brooke Pickering	5'4" x 7'2"	20th Century
61°	Beni Ouarain Cape	Peter Davies	3'2" x 6'8"	20th Century
62°	Beni Ouarain Cape	Jefferson S. Hyde	2'10" x 7'6"	20th Century
63	Beni Ouarain Cape	I.M.A.[2]	2'9" x 6'2"	20th Century
64	Beni Ouarain Cape	Linda Lawrence	2'10" x 5'10"	20th Century
65	Beni Ouarain Cape	Alf & Judi Taylor	3'2" x 6'8"	20th Century
66	Azrou Saddle Bags	Private Collection	1'4" x 3'9"	20th Century
67	Beni M'Guild Pillow	James F. Jereb	1'4" x 2'6"	20th Century

Notes

[°]Illustrated   [1]American Museum of Moroccan Art   [2]Indianapolis Museum of Art   [3]Tazenakht

Bibliography

James F. Jereb, Ph.D.

Bazinet, Michael "Corsairs, Commerce and Cognomens." in Oriental Rug Review, Vol. 11 Number 4, pp. 17-20, 1991

Bernes, J.P. et Jacob A. Arts et objects du Maroc, Meubles Zellidjs, Tapis, Paris ABC Decor. 1974

Besancenot, J. Costumes et Types du Maroc, Paris: Les Horizons de France, 1940

Bovill, E.W. The Golden Trade of the Moors, London: Oxford University Press, 1968

Collingwood, Peter The Techniques of Rug Weaving, New York: Watson-Guptill Publisher, 1969

Davis, Susan "Continuity and Change: Handwoven Textiles in Fes, Morocco." in Oriental Rug Review, Vol. 11 Number 4, pp. 21-27, 1991

Fiske, Patricia, Pickering, W. Russell and Yohe, Ralph ed. From the Far West: Carpets and Textiles from Morocco, Washington, D.C. The Textile Museum, 1980

Flint, Bert Tapis, Tissages, Vol. 2 of Formes et Symboles dans les arts maghrebins, Tangier: Imprimie E.M.I., 1974

Forelli, Sally and Jeanette Harries "Traditional Berber Weaving in Central Morocco." The Textile Museum Journal, Vol. 4 Number 4, pp. 41-60., 1977

Fraser, David "Weft Twined Rugs and Related Textiles of North Africa and the Middle East." in Oriental Rug Review, Vol. 11 Number 4, pp. 30-39, 1991

Gallotti, Jean Les tapis marocains, Paris: Librarie Centrale des Beaux-Arts., 1919 "Weaving and Dyeing in North Africa." in CIBA Review, May 1939, Number 21, pp. 738-761

Gilfoy, Peggy Stolz Fabrics in Celebration from the Collection, Indianapolis: Indianapolis Museum of Art., 1983

Golvin, Lucien Aspects de l'artisanant en Afrique du Nord, Paris Presses Universitaire de France, 1967

Jereb, James F. "Tradition, Design and Magic: Moroccan Tribal Weaves." in Hali, August, Issue 52, pp. 112-121, 1990.

Justin, Valerie "Shawls of the Berbers of Atlas Mountains." in Oriental Rug Review, Volume 11, Number 4, pp. 40-41, 1991

continued on the next page

Kiewe, Heinz Edgar Ancient Berber Tapestries and Rugs and Ancient Moroccan Embroideries, Oxford: Maison Francaise., 1952

Laroui, Abdallah History of the Maghrib, Princeton: Princeton University Press

Mather, Vanessa Women and Property in Morocco, London: Cambridge University Press

Mernissi, Fatima Doing Daily Battle, trans. by Mary Jo Lakeland, London: Women Press Ltd.

Montagne, Robert The Berbers, London: Frank Cass and Co. Ltd., 1973

Paine, Sheila Embroidered Textiles: Traditional Patterns from Five Continents, New York: Rizzoli, 1990

Pascon, Paul Le Haouz du Marrakech, Rabat: Tangier, 1977

Pickering, Brooke, Pickering W. Russell, Yohe, Ralph "Rug Collecting in Morocco." in Oriental Rug Review, Volume 11, Number 4, pp. 11-15, 1991

Picton, John and Mack, John African Textiles, London: British Museum Publications, Ltd; London, England, 1979

Reswick, Irmtraud Traditional Textiles of Tunisia and Related North African Weavings, Los Angeles: Craft and Folk Art Museum., 1985

Revault, Jacques Le Tissage et le tatouage dans le Moyen Atlas, Fes, Marocains., 1933

Richard, Prosper Tapis de Rabat, Vol. 1 of Corpus du Tapis Marocains, Paris: Librarie Orientaliste Paul Geuthner, 1923
    Tapis du Moyen Atlas, Vol. 2 of Corpus des Tapis Marocains, Paris: Librarie Orientaliste Paul Geuthner, 1926
    Tapis du Haut Atlas et du Haouz de Marrakech, Vol. 3 of Corpus des Tapis Marocains, Paris: Librarie Orientaliste Paul Geuthner, 1927.
    Tapis Marocains, Paris: Office Marocain due Tourisme et Office Cherfien de controle et d'exportation, 1932

Sefrioui, Ahmed African Costumes and Attire: Morocco, Rabat: Gerard-Guibert, 1982

Sijelmassi, Mohammed Les Arts traditionnels au Maroc, Paris: Avenir Graphique, 1974

Stone, Caroline The Embroideries of North Africa, London: Longman, 1985

Taylor, Alf A Treasure Hunter's Guide to Morocco, Scenic Publications, Tuscon, Az., 1991.

Terasse, Henri, et Hainaut, J. Les Arts decoratifs au Maroc, Paris: Henri Laurens Editeur, 1925

Turnbull, Patrick Black Barbary, London: Hurst and Blackett, 1939.

Westermarck, Edward A Ritual and Belief in Morocco, in 2 Volumes, Hyde Park, N.Y.: University Books, 1968

James F. Jereb, Ph.D., *Santa Fe, New Mexico, has spent years in Morocco studying tribal arts and has written extensively on Moroccan carpets and North African arts and textiles.*